God Speaks

Prophetic Words and Visions from Abba's Heart

Vol. II

Edie Bayer

Available in This Series:

God Speaks: Prophetic Words
and Visions from Abba's Heart
Vol. I and Vol. II
ISBN-13: 978-1-946106-26-1
ISBN-13: 978-1-946106-27-8

Other books by Edie Bayer:

Spiritual Espionage: Going Undercover for the Kingdom of God!
Power Thieves: 7 Spirits that Steal Your Power, and How to Get it Back!
Spiritual Lightning Rods Connected to the Father of Lights
Narco: Awake O' Sleeper
Write That Book! You Have a Book in You – Now Write It!
Book and Workbook

CD's and DVD's
Salt – Cd/Dvd
Write That Book! – Cd/Dvd

http://KingdomPromoters.org/books_cds.html

Watch our Author Seminar Online 24/7:
http://KingdomPromoters.org/writerclass.html

DEDICATION

This two-book series is dedicated to the Lord.
Without Him these books would not be.

GOD SPEAKS, VOL. II

CONTENTS

GOD SPEAKS, VOL. II

ACKNOWLEDGMENTS

Thank you to all who love the Lord and long to hear His voice.
You are His greatest treasures!

GOD SPEAKS, VOL. II

CHAPTER ONE

REMOVE THE BULB

God tends to speak to me through common, everyday events, and sometimes some that are not-so-common! As an example, our refrigerator door has a computerized water dispenser. A few days ago, it started flashing at us and yesterday finally stopped working altogether. Since I am a "Do-It-Yourself-er", I started looking for parts to fix it. I had already found a part to fix our dishwasher, so I should be able to do it on a refrigerator, right? I mean, God is no respecter of persons, so why should I be one of appliances?

I noted the model number and jumped online. The very first place I found had schematics, but nothing that referred to our specific issue. Undeterred, I went back to the search engine, and re-entered the model number again. A whole list of sites came up, one of which had reviews for various electrical components that fixed problems similar to what we were experiencing.

Reading through the reviews for these parts, I became progressively more convinced that there could be a multitude of things wrong. One review said it could be this part, and another that part, but someone else said it might be this other part. After reading three or four of them, and I was convinced that the problem was too difficult and expensive for me to do myself, I came across a really short review which read simply…

"Seems that old bulbs draw too much current and cause the control panel to fail in sending signal to icemaker motor. Removing the bulb cured this fault and the control panel worked fine."

I sat back in my chair. Could it really be that simple? Removing the light bulb? The parts I had looked at could total hundreds of dollars and hours of sweating labor, even fixing it myself. A light bulb?

I went to the refrigerator, and realized I didn't even know WHERE to look for the bulb! I saw the lighted dots on the computer panel that indicate whether it was water or ice, and thought, "That is going to be difficult to get to the bulb!" Still investigating, I looked INSIDE the water dispenser housing. Sure enough, a lightbulb! I grabbed it and untwisted it, and pulled it out. It was ugly, nasty and dirty. Out of habit, I checked the filament inside the bulb. Surprisingly, it was intact. I sat it down on the counter, and prepared to test this "repair". I grabbed a water glass and lo and behold – we had water! I tested the crushed ice, the ice cube dispenser and the water once more … and all were working, just as they should, the way they were intended.

So, what is the moral to this twenty-first century parable? Read it again, and see if your light bulb comes on! The review said, "Seems that old bulbs draw too much current and cause the control panel to fail in sending signal to icemaker motor. Removing the bulb cured this fault and the control panel worked fine."

Here's what I believe God was saying. Most of us are familiar with the "lightbulb over the head" as a symbol for an idea or a thought process. I believe He was speaking to us about our OLD thought patterns and the way we deal with the spiritual realm. The old ideas and thought processes are short-circuiting what He wants for us! I believe He wants us to interact both with Him and with the spiritual realm in a brand new way – to get a new idea – a new bulb!

We are His modern day dispensers of His water! If we are not working properly, the whole system comes to a grinding halt. Here is what He showed me:

The old bulbs — our old thought processes, our old ideas, our old ways of doing things and interacting with both God's Kingdom and the demonic realm. Things of tradition (Luke 11:42-44) and old mindsets that get in our way (John 3:3-12).

Draw too much current — they are taking up way too much of our time and energy! We need to look forward to see what God is doing now and quit trying to do it "like it's always been done". We must refocus our energy into how God is doing it now, in the new – in the CURRENT!

Cause the control panel to fail — WE ARE THE CONTROL PANEL! Church of God, YOU are the control panel! We have the authority, given to us by Jesus in John 17 and seen in Hebrews 2 and Matthew 28! All of creation groans for us to be revealed, even to ourselves (Rom. 8:22)!

In sending signal to icemaker motor — We need to get the "right now" signal, and move on it! We are a MACHINE – the body of Christ, a living organism. The motor of this machine needs to get the correct signals to go in our God-intended direction. When our signal is short-circuited we wander about as lost sheep without a shepherd (Matt. 9:36).

The solution is incredibly easy! *First, realize you have a special "model number" assigned by God!* You were created for such a time as this (Esther 4:14) and that model number was built to work in this season. You have a "now assignment". Your old one is finished. You must receive a new, clear signal and directions for this new assignment!

3

Second, recognize there may be a problem with your control panel: your thought processes. Be open to receive instruction and any necessary course correction as a true son (Hebrews 12:7).

Third, don't let the enemy lie to you! Just as several reviews led me to believe that the repair on my water dispenser would be elaborate and expensive, the fix was incredibly easy! Don't let any human being or demon from hell tell you that your issue is too deep or too hard or too complex, or worse, it will never go away.

Fourth, don't be deterred or discouraged! If these steps don't fix it immediately, go back to the source. Just as I didn't find my solution during the first search, your solution may take a little more seeking. But don't get discouraged! It's all spiritual, and can be remedied with just your mouth and your faith! It's THAT simple! Are you ready?

REMOVE THE BULB. Get rid of it! Pull it out! This thought process is a murderous tool designed to destroy you, a plot and plan of the enemy to keep you from moving forward! This includes racism, sexism, pride, victim mentality and a host of others. Ask Holy Spirit to search your heart (Ps. 139:23) and reveal to you what is short-circuiting your system. Then repent and move on into your future.

REMOVE IT! Don't "get used to it" – get rid of it! Recognize it for what it is, a snare and a trap! Most health issues, marital problems, gender identity issues, spending issues…they are all rooted in the spiritual realm. As such, they can be solved on your knees, in the spiritual realm. You are a disciple of Jesus, so ask Holy Spirit to teach you how to pray (Luke 11:1-13) about this particular issue – then do it!

REMOVE IT! Realize you "may" be under spiritual attack because you are! It's not happening to you strictly in the natural. It's the "natural" manifesting the spiritual realm! Fight the war spiritually, not carnally (2 Cor. 10:4). Your weapons of warfare are in the spirit. Get your angels back on the job. They have been waiting to hear from you!

REMOVE IT! Remove that religious spirit from your midst! Get over the "old way", the way it's always been done, the way we used to dress, the way we used to look, or smell or sound, or talk or preach or sing! Just recently I bucked God when He told me to wear jeans and tennis shoes to a meeting. He told me I had a religious spirit that was telling me I was required to dress up!

REMOVE IT! Remove the thought pattern that God can only speak in certain ways, and He cannot in others. Forget all that! I was in Matthew 6 and I actually HEARD the voice of God speaking to me from the Mount. I was in another dimension with Him and heard Him speaking to me personally. Don't limit God!

Once you remove the bulb, test the waters! They should be flowing again freely. If they are not, go back to Step 1 – Ask God! God requires that His rivers flow without restraint. He knows where the obstacles and the hazards are in your life. Don't wait until your unit stops working completely. Trust Him implicitly to know how to fix your water dispenser, and let Him do it!

CHAPTER TWO

REJOICE! THE ENEMY'S HAND HAS BEEN OVERTURNED!

As I was coming out of sleep this morning, I heard, "THE ENEMY'S HAND HAS BEEN OVERTURNED"! I got a quick vision of soil being tilled, or "turned-over". The soil was rich and brown, and I saw a close-up of one of the furrows that had already been made in it. In that moment, I also felt as though new seed had already been planted. I felt the anticipation of this new seed coming to fruition! A fresh harvest!

Annually, farmers till weeds under, by turning the soil OVER. This kills the weeds and buries their seeds, inhibiting them from growing back. The Lord spoke to me in PAST TENSE when He said that the enemy's hand has been overturned! This is important because it means we are not waiting for it ... it has already happened! His crop of weeds has been buried and killed off! This is good news, people of God! It is finished!

Listen! Just yesterday, a friend shared a prophetic word about curses over America being broken. I truly believe THIS IS THAT – a time when the old weeds and seeds have been overturned and tilled under! I believe that judgements against us have been overturned. I believe this is a time when the curses *that have already been broken* start to manifest themselves as freedom from the chains of their bondage! I believe that this is a time that we will long remember – a time of the enemy's hand being shown as having been lifted off of America and off all of our lives -- individually and corporately!

The enemy has been buried!

I believe it is a TWO FOLD process:

1. I believe, if we follow what God is saying, is that He - the God of all the universe - has buried the enemy ... under the very soil that he was using to grow his crop of destruction!

Do you remember the story of Ai in Joshua 8:22? In this story, and I will paraphrase, the army of the city of Ai *was led to believe* it was chasing the Israelites out of town, when in fact, it was a holy-ghost setup and God turned the tables on Ai! The city's army was sandwiched, and it fell into its own trap.

Do you see? God has turned the tables (and the soil!) on the enemy, just like He did at Ai! It may LOOK LIKE the enemy has the upper hand, even right now, this minute....but I believe God is only leading him on! I believe that you will see that what was trying to chase you will end up turning back on itself – creating chaos in the enemy's camp for your victory! God has overturned the enemy's hand!

"Do not be deceived: God cannot be mocked. Whatever a man sows, he will reap in return (Galatians 6:7)." God cannot be mocked! That strong, leafy tree bough that was torn off by the high winds only LOOKS like it is still alive! It is indeed dead, feeding on itself and what little strength still remains. The enemy of our soul is exactly the same! Fear not for he is a defeated foe!
"Fear not, *little flock*, for it is your Father's good pleasure to give you the kingdom (Luke 12:32)."

A fresh crop is on the way!

2. I felt as though new seed had been sown into already prepared soil, and the anticipation of the fresh crop was exhilarating!

You know all that heartache, sorrow, toil and pain you have gone through, maybe even as recently as yesterday? I believe it was preparing your soil, the soil of your heart, for the new seed and the fresh, victorious crop! All the pain, strife, division, anger and WARFARE that you have encountered has turned you into the warrior that the Lord always intended for you to be!

The rocks have been dug out of your soul. You have learned to overcome! You have learned to forgive, to submit, to follow and to lead! You are now a fully equipped soldier. Your soil has been prepared. Your heart is right, both with man and with God. You are ready to harvest the new, fresh crop!

What is this new, fresh harvest?

Amos 9:13 states, *"Behold, the days are coming,"* declares the *LORD, "when the plowman shall overtake the reaper and the treader of grapes him who sows the seed; the mountains shall drip sweet wine, and all the hills shall flow with it."*

We have seen the plowman. We have seen the reaper. We have seen the grape treaders and we have seen the one who sows the seed…but we have never seen the mountains drip with sweet wine, nor all the hills flow with it!

What does that look like, exactly? I would venture to say that no one really knows for sure, but we all will know by the Spirit – it is our NEW, FRESH HARVEST! It is something that we have NEVER seen before! It is something that is so new, and so fresh, that it will take our breath away, awestruck as we gaze upon its beauty!

I believe that each of us will know our fresh harvest when we get there, as it is revealed to us. It will be completely different from anything that we have experienced up until now. I will say this: I believe that you have been uniquely prepared for this moment, and it is upon us. Everything that you have been through has prepared you for this time in humanity's history. You are uniquely qualified to fulfill this purpose. No one else has the calling that you do for such a time as this (Esther 4:14)!

God has saved the best wine for last! He did it at Cana (John 2:1-11) and He is doing it again. Get ready to drink deeply. His mountains are now dripping with it, and you will soon be flowing with it, too!

CHAPTER THREE

BREAKING THROUGH THE SHAKING: GOD'S G-FORCE

In prayer this morning, I was sitting on the edge of my bed. The Lord began to show me visions of mountaintops and beautiful country vistas from a high elevation. I was passing both over them and through them simultaneously. I asked the Lord, "Are you showing me something here or am I flying?" He responded to me that He was showing me my destiny!

The realization hit: **God takes us the furthest when we move the least!** God gave me several thoughts in rapid succession: "God shows us things with our eyes closed!" and "We travel great distances on our knees!" Then the Lord reminded me, **"Be Still and Know that IAM God (Ps. 46:10)."**

Suddenly, He showed me a vision of sitting in an airplane, buckled into my seat and very still, thousands of feet in the air, travelling at hundreds of feet per minute, and yet not even feeling it. Immediately, He showed me another vision, astronauts in outer space, floating around in their ship with no gravity. He reminded me that even though their bodies appear to not be moving, their spacecraft is travelling tens of thousands of feet per second – and yet, there is no gravity to hold them in place.

Break Loose of the Earth's Gravitational Pull!

This is when the Lord spoke a word that just rocked my world: "Break loose of the earth's gravitational pull!"

He showed me an astronaut buckled into his seat, in his space suit with his helmet on. His entire body was shaking, his face grimacing in pain with the G-force and the pressure of breaking out of the earth's gravitational pull. His body was shaking, his seat was shaking, the entire ship was shaking and quaking! This meant that *before he could enter the calm of deep space with no gravity, e*verything that could be shaken was shaking (Hebrews 12:27)!

Here is what I believe God is saying to us today: Come up here (Rev. 4:1 and Rev. 11:12)! Not just once, but twice, and He is saying something different each time! Whenever God says something twice in the scriptures, He wants us to really get it and pay attention. You need to get this, so pay attention!

In Revelation 4:1 the Lord spoke to us and said, **"Come up here, and I will show you what must take place after this."** He wants to show us things to come (John 16:13). He wants to give us a roadmap for the nation. He wants to instruct us and guide us into the impending REVIVAL. Yes, He wants to talk to us and have fellowship with us, but this is different. This kind of strategic spiritual mapping can only happen on a higher level – on HIS level. We simply cannot do it at this level, the first heaven, with our earthly mindsets. We MUST go up to Him!

There is a shaking as the spaceman and the ship climb higher and higher, to break free of the pull of the earth's atmosphere. You should expect that too! That is why every time you intentionally try to go higher with God, or sit still in one place to speak to the Lord and attempt to leave the earth's atmosphere, hell's minions show up. Their job is to stop you, trip you up, shake you up or at bare minimum slow you down. They know what is at stake.

Everything that can be shaken will be shaken.

Everything that can be shaken will be shaken (Heb. 12:27). You must break through the shaking! The enemy doesn't want you to spend time or go higher with God. Just as the astronaut must go through the tremendous pain and pressure of breaking through the earth's atmosphere, so you must go through the shaking to reach the calm of deep space where God exists! You need to endure the shaking to enjoy the promotion.

The religious spirits, the nay-sayers and the haters *will show up* to complete their demonic assignments. It has already started. People will tell you what you are doing is wrong, or 'that can't be God!' Some may even tell you that it is HERESY. The religious walls are coming down, and we are taking ourselves out of the battle. We simply go up to meet with God. The enemy cannot go where God takes us for these strategic planning sessions, and they cannot win against the war that the Almighty wages. The enemy got kicked out of heaven, and God didn't change His mind!

The G-Force of the craft leaving the earth's atmosphere exceeds the amount of pressure that the human body can endure, so the astronaut must wear a special suit. God is so smart that He gave us one, too! We live and move and breathe IN THE HOLY SPIRIT! **"'For in Him we *live and move and have our being*'** (Acts 17:28)." God knew the shaking was coming. He knows the amount of pressure that this generation will have to endure to break through! He gave us a specially made suit to put on - our Holy Spirit! He wants us to not only make sure that we will survive the shaking - but to actually THRIVE in it! He wants us to thrive in the G-Force...IN His GOD-FORCE!

When I saw what He was saying about the God Force – breaking free of gravity to join Him in the heavenlies – I realized that when we "come up here", we break free of the GRAVE. Gravity pulls you down while God lifts you up! **"Come up here, and I will show you what must take place *AFTER THIS*** (emphasis mine)." **AFTER THIS** for us are heavenly places, and Jesus holds all the keys! He wants to show us things on the other side of open doors that simply cannot be seen down here. We MUST go to Him, and meet Him in the clouds! God exists on the *other side* of the cross, on the *other side* of the grave! When we break through gravity to reach God, enduring and overcoming the shaking, we overcome the grave of this earthly realm! We can function on this side getting our war plans and strategies from the *other side* straight from the Lord of Armies! Come on Christians! Break through the shaking!

There is a second reason to "come up here" in Revelation 11:12... **"Then they heard a loud voice from heaven saying to them, "Come up here." And they went up to heaven in a cloud, while their enemies looked on."** When you push through to break through the shaking, endure the pressure, and use the God-Force that He has given you to reach Him you will beat every obstacle. You will overcome every demon, every curse, every hex and every assignment against you. It will not matter whether it is witchcraft, voodoo, demonic, generational or any other type of bomb from below.

When this happens, all your enemy can do is WATCH. That's right! He is, and they are, totally powerless to do anything about it! When God says your trouble is over, it's OVER! When God gives you a strategy from the *other side* there is nothing that anybody can do on this side to stop it!

"Do not conform to the pattern of this world, but be transformed by the renewing of your mind (Romans

12:2)" "And the peace of God, which surpasses all comprehension, will guard your hearts and your minds in Christ Jesus (Phil. 4:7)."

Break loose of the earth's gravitational pull! Change your mind (Rom. 12:2)! Don't get sucked down into the lower, base, everyday thought processes of life. Think on higher things (Phil. 4:8-9). Make going up Mt. Zion a priority! Breathe life back into your prayer life! Spend time with God! Go with Him to the places that He longs to take you, to show you all things He wants to do with you. He wants to lead you and guide you into all truth (John 16:13). He wants to show you your destiny! He wants you to fly over mountaintops and lush valleys with Him, and join Him on spiritual adventures as He takes you on your own journeys and travels with Him.

Go higher and break through the shaking with God's G-Force! He will give you the strategies you need!

CHAPTER FOUR

JESUS IS TAKING CENTER STAGE!

As I was praying for President Trump this morning I went into a vision. I heard Jesus say, "You have plenty of word in you. You need to have some fun!" Jesus reached out to me with a golden mechanical arm, like the arm of the Iron Man suit, and grabbed ahold of my hand, pulling me up where He is.

I found myself sitting on a tree bough, side by side with Jesus, swinging my legs like a kid. We were sitting above a line of horse-drawn wagons. They were similar to stagecoaches, wooden, but not the covered variety. The path they were driving down was directly under the tree where I was seated with Jesus on the tree bough, but on the other side of the tree trunk. Looking down, it was dusty and unclear, kind of "grayed out". I could see somewhat the line of wagons that were proceeding under the tree, but not very clearly.

I thought of Zaccheus climbing into a tree to see Him (Luke 19:1-10). His name means clean and pure, such as the first pressing of the olives to make Extra-Virgin olive oil. I wondered if he stood up and searched for Jesus, or if he sat on a tree bough as I was doing now, waiting for the Lord to come.

Jesus asked me what I saw, and I responded, "Nothing really."

He told me to look further down the line of passing wagons. I looked out into the distance and saw a horse, very clearly, a golden colored farm horse pulling one of the wagons. It had a hat on, complete with a daisy! We've all seen this image at some time. I'd never contemplated why the horse had the hat on before, other than to look cute. However, it suddenly hit me that the horse was wearing the hat to shield its eyes from the sun…it was protection!

Immediately after that vision, I was transported. I saw myself standing in an arena, preaching, as a whitish well-trained circus horse was circling around me with no rider. Its trainer stood behind me with a long whip in the center of the arena. I then saw the same horse circling the arena, but this time it had a circus rider ballerina on it and no trainer. Suddenly, it was me on the horse circling the arena. First I was standing up and preaching as the horse circled the arena, then sitting down and preaching, still with my microphone in my hand.

I heard Jesus say, "Forget everything you've ever known and prepare for the ride of your life. Don't be like the Israelites who wandered in the desert for forty years. Put down that mindset and get anew, get renewed. Leave all that other stuff behind!

"Come up here on this tree bough and get higher with me. Look down on what is going on. You have discernment, use it. You can see from a higher perspective when you are seated with me in high places.

"It's emotions that drag you down into the earth realm. You cannot see the forest for the trees when you are emotional. Step back and see from a distance what is going on in any particular circumstance.

"The enemy uses your emotions and pushes your buttons. You

have to know that and ACT, do not REACT! Pray for people that they respond and do not react. There will be many opportunities to react in the days to come.

"Respond from a higher position of authority, a higher position of enlightenment. Do not react like a brute beast. Your hat will shield you from the things that make you emotional and make emotional decisions, even eating emotionally."

Here's the good news! I believe that Jesus is giving us a "new hat" to wear! Just like the horse in my vision wore a hat as protection from the blazing sun, this "new hat" will be one that protects us from the elements that would affect our mind, will and emotions. He wants us OUT of the earth realm, UP on that tree bough with Him, looking DOWN on the things of this world. We were made to rule and reign from above, not from this level - this earthly plane!

The wagons and the horses are symbols of pioneering and blazing new trails, new paths, and having fun while we do it, victoriously and with authority! Although in my vision it was "grayed out" and dusty, and not very clear right now as I looked at the wagons directly underneath me, as I look a little further down the path, it becomes clear! We carry the supply that the world needs in our wagons – JESUS! We have an unprecedented opportunity to blaze new paths, pioneer new trails and do new things to bring Jesus to a lost and dying world.

I also believe that the Lord is giving us the opportunity to do things that have never been done while preaching the gospel. In my vision, He initially had me in the arena while the horse with the trainer and then the circus rider entertained the crowd. This symbolically stood for Christians not being "the main event", so to speak, but we were there in the background, even underground in some instances. I believe God is changing this! In my vision, God moved me ONTO the horse, both standing and sitting, preaching the Gospel, as the horse circled the arena. This to me means that He is MOVING US INTO THE MAIN ARENA, into the limelight – *we are becoming the main event!* HIS WORD is becoming the main event! Jesus is taking center stage!

This is important for many reasons! It is easy to get lost in the background, in the midst of "white noise" in this world. It is entirely different when God's Word and His ministries shine in the limelight. We now have a President who is "UN-Persecuting" Christians! He is bringing us once again into the limelight! We will be able to preach the Gospel, OPENLY, unlike the last several years. We will no longer be in the background, the "silent majority". Instead, we will openly rule and reign in this country, and as the USA goes, so goes the world!

Initially I was standing on the horse as I preached, then I was seated. I believe that initially we will have to "STAND UP" for what we believe, but as time goes on, we will take a seat and "settle in" to what is God's will and our inheritance...FREEDOM! Experiencing Jesus is freedom!

One example of this is that the foothold that we have in Hollywood will increase exponentially in the next short while. I believe that our toehold will become a bonafide stance, a Christian movement! I believe that we will see more and more Christian movies coming out, proclaiming and declaring the Gospel of Jesus Christ. Some of these movies will become even more mainstream than what we have seen to date. Furthermore, I believe some "closet Christian" movie stars will start coming out of the closet, now that it is politically possible! Some of these Christian movie stars will take a stand for purity, and justice, and they will make being Christian "cool"! It will be fashionable to be pure, and holy, unlike before. Instead of Hollywood, I believe it will henceforth be known as HOLY-Would!

I believe that holiness will spill over into ALL the arts and sciences, government, family – in fact, I believe that God is taking back His mountains – all SEVEN of them!

God is doing a new thing all over the world! He desires that we take our position "on the tree bough" with Him, seated at His side, in high places, in heavenly places. Ask Him for your "new hat", the one that will shield you from the barbs of the enemy that are aimed at your soul to push the buttons of your emotions. This new hat will guard your heart, "…for out of it flows the issues of life (Proverbs 4:23)." Get ready to ride your horse and take your wagon to new territory for the glory of God, be center stage, and enjoy every minute of it!

In this unprecedented time in history, the GO-BUTTON has finally been pushed. Let's Go!

CHAPTER FIVE
WHEN THE HOLY SPIRIT
COMES IN LIKE A FLOOD

Has your washing machine ever overflowed? Mine did today. A few days ago, it was unbalanced in the spin cycle, and started "walking" across the room. My husband moved it back, but the drain hose had partially come out of the wall, and he didn't see it. So when it went into the drain cycle today, water went everywhere! We had a bona fide flood! The water ran through the door of the utility room and under the wall into my front room, flowing toward the front door.

I had been making preparations to house fourteen traveling ministers this weekend. I was busily cleaning house, making beds and doing laundry. Simultaneously, I was editing a book, ministering and making plans for upcoming events, making a shopping list for animal feed, as well as necessities for remodeling our kitchen pantry. I had many balls in the air, trying to juggle them all simultaneously. So, when I walked into the front room to face the flood on the floor, I almost panicked! I knew the floor needed to be mopped, but not today! I was too busy!

I would have given anything for a squeegee! I grabbed a bunch of towels and threw them down to create a "dam" and to start to soak up the water. I had the thought, "Now I will have to do another load of towels!" This is exactly what created this flood to begin with.

As I was cleaning up this monumental, Noah-style mess, the Holy Spirit started to show me some things. While He was speaking, I realized that there was a lesson in this for us all.

I don't know about you, but our utility room is a hardworking room in our house. It is part laundromat, part storage shed, and part chicken-hatching-chick-brooder area. It is a multi-tasking room. We have a second refrigerator and our freezer in there too, not to mention a whole cast of items that we only use occasionally. These were tucked away, hidden in the corners of the room...you know, "out of sight, out of mind". As I pulled them all out, one after the other, mopping up the flood from our tile floors, the Holy Spirit spoke to me. He simply said, *"WHEN The Holy Spirit comes in like a flood..."*

My bible says, **"When the enemy comes in like a flood, The Spirit of the LORD will lift up a standard against him** (Isaiah 59:19)." We all know that scripture, but years ago I heard it preached otherwise. The Holy Spirit confirmed it to me today.

I heard it preached that *the comma is in the wrong place,* and that passage of scripture should read, "When the enemy comes in, *LIKE A FLOOD, THE SPIRIT OF THE LORD WILL LIFT UP A STANDARD AGAINST HIM* (emphasis mine)." See? That is what I believe the Holy Spirit was saying to me today. That He is coming in like a flood against the enemy! And as He does, He will simultaneously **UNCOVER** and **CLEANSE** what it is that He reveals – like a flood!

I had a "cleansing" dream a few nights ago. Cleansing dreams usually involve toilets or showers. If we are fortunate, we are alone in the dream. In my instance, it was in my front yard and in the neighbor's yard! So, I knew some cleansing was coming – but I didn't know that He meant LITERALLY!

Now, as I was mopping up the mess with my many bath towels, Holy Spirit showed me a number of things that He is cleansing in this time in our lives, *beginning with me*:

1. **Things that are tucked away and "hidden"** in the corners: We have a wide variety of things in our utility room, things that we almost never use. There is an extra vacuum cleaner and a dehumidifier, some wire shelving, and numerous other items "hidden" and "tucked away", things we only pull out and use every once in a while. Holy Spirit showed me that these equate to ACTIONS and ATTITUDES that we have.

   What are some things that YOU only pull out and use occasionally? Does a "censored" word "just slip out" every once in a while? Do you "bite" when you get mad, however rarely? Are you racist? Do you get drunk? The Holy Spirit will be working on these attitudes in His children! God's people MUST walk virtuously, because HOLINESS = WHOLENESS! We need to be WHOLE in order to walk through the days to come!

2. **Dirt**: The Holy Spirit showed me all the dirt that was piled up in the corners of my utility room, under the washing machine and the sink. I was ashamed! There is lots of dirt that we don't ordinarily see, because it is hidden behind, and under, these items that we so seldomly pull out and use! Holy Spirit showed me that this DIRT is the UNDERLYING CAUSES OF OUR ACTIONS AND THOUGHT PROCESSES!

   What kind of DIRT do you have hidden? As an example, there was a man who drank himself to sleep every year on Super Bowl Sunday because he lost his daughter one year during the game. Ironically, she was hit by a drunk driver, and he never forgave himself for her death. His UNFORGIVENESS punished him, year after year.

Another example is when someone "snaps" at us, or is vicious, it's because we have unwittingly walked into their unhealed WOUND. They "bite" back, because it hurts! This means that they (okay, WE) simply need healing! Holy Spirit, our Comforter and our Guide will lead us into all truth (John 16:15)! People who were abused in some way, whether physically, emotionally or verbally usually carry shame. He wants us healed of all that!

He will show us WHAT we need to be healed of, and the very best way to get healed, so that we don't have these characteristics anymore.

3. **Irregularities in the foundation:** There were puddles of standing water on different areas of the tile floor in my front room. There were high areas that the water had flowed over, seeking lower ground. The floor slants a little, too, because it used to be the front porch before we closed it in and made it our front room and home church space. Our house was built many years ago, and although the owner/builder was a decent carpenter, our foundation is not perfectly flat. As a result, as I was moving the water, using the towel as a squeegee, the Holy Spirit showed me the irregularities in our house's foundation. Holy Spirit showed me that these IRREGULARITIES are faulty belief systems that we have acquired in our walk. We have some GOOD beliefs, but we do not have All Truth!

What kind of IRREGULARITIES do you have in your foundation in "your house"? Do you think that God is mad at you? Or worse, that He gave you a disease? Do you only go to church on Sundays? Do you always tithe and give offerings? I am not judging anyone. I am simply implying that there may be some "cracks" in your foundation! God is a "foundation God". He will give you foundational beliefs, and build upon them. He cannot build on a faulty foundation!

You must know that the Holy Spirit will be seeking to level out ALL the high places in your walk with the Lord. He will simultaneously be seeking to fill in all the low spots. Holy Spirit is looking to train you up properly. He will make sure that your foundation is SOLID so that God can continue to build upon it, precept upon precept (see Isaiah 28:10).

4. **House looks solid, but there are gaps under the walls**: As the water was trying to find the lowest possible level, it also seeped into the closet in the next room, which fortunately was also tile. Because there are irregularities in the foundation, the wall doesn't make full contact with the floor. It appears to be solid, but there are gaps under the wall. The Holy Spirit showed me these GAPS will cause issues in our walk.

Do things just "LOOK GOOD" on the outside? I know some people for whom "appearances are everything"! They would never let you know that there is something wrong with their perfectly projected world. When asked, they are always, "Blessed and highly favored!" I would like to propose that God wants us to walk in TRUTH, all of it – the Good, the Bad and the Ugly. He already knows it! So who are we hiding it from?

Even though your wall (walk) looks solid, if there are gaps between it and your foundation, you will eventually have structural issues! A building can only go as high as its foundation allows. Allow the Holy Spirit to build and rebuild your foundation! Allow the Holy Spirit to come in and fill in the gaps! Let Him teach you what you do not know, the things that you will need to get to the next level. Let Him work on you to change your mindsets and preconceived notions of what the Kingdom Age truly is supposed to be! Learn to lean on other believers, because iron sharpens iron (see Proverbs 27:17). Get involved in a community of believing believers!

5. **Things are out of place**, just when I thought I was done: I finally got all the water mopped up and drained out the front door. Turning around, I saw two, large plastic tubs with my husband's music books in them. They don't belong in the front room, but they had not made it to their permanent home yet because they are large and heavy. I moved them, and underneath was more water! I still wasn't done. The Holy Spirit showed me that there are some things that are currently in our lives that He is still working on – in my life and yours.

    What in your life is out of place, something that doesn't belong where it is? The key here is to look at your life through the lens of the Holy Spirit, because that is exactly what He is doing. He looks at our lives, at the things that do not belong there, and He gently nudges us to move them, or helps us to remove them. He is already at work in you. He is already working on revealing and cleansing those thoughts and attitudes, those people and circumstances, those issues, and helping to move them out of your life. If you have not been able to move them, because they are too large and too heavy, like my husband's tubs of music books, fret not! The Holy Spirit is incredibly strong! All things are possible for those who believe (Mark 9:23)! Just believe.

6. The Amplified says, **"And we know [with great confidence] that God [who is deeply concerned about us] causes all things to work together [as a plan] for good for those who love God, to those who are called according to His plan *and* purpose."** It turned out that the flood water made the room smell great! It was all fresh and

clean, from the washing of the water of the Word (see Ephesians 5:26). The Holy Spirit breathed on me today through this set of unfortunate circumstances, which He turned around for my good, and YOURS! He gave us all a lesson today, through this message. The Holy Spirit showed me that His Water cleanses with the word. It makes everything smell fresh and great!

If something in your life "stinks", call on the Holy Spirit! He is here to assist. He is your paraclete, Him Who comes alongside, your helper, your comforter. He is the Spirit of the Lord! Jesus sent Him to us to help us, to lead us and guide us into all truth. He is our helper. Lean on Him! He will be more than happy to point you to Jesus and glorify the Father! Just like today!

7. **The cleansing is a continuous process**: Even now I see two little puddles of water by the front door....

Blessings in your cleansings!

CHAPTER SIX

SPIRITUAL SAFETY INSTRUCTIONS:
ARE YOU PREPARED?

I was on an airplane recently. As usual, at the beginning of the flight, the flight attendants went through their little "safety-spiel", telling us about oxygen masks and exit signs. I have heard it so many times I really just watch and listen out of courtesy. As I listened, I looked around the cabin. I couldn't help but notice that very few people, other than me, were paying attention. I thought to myself, "God help us if anything happens! I hope they can open the exit door!"

The guy in front of me was a big guy, and he had his seat leaned back. The man next to me in the middle seat was a big guy, too. He was using both arm rests. Feeling a little squeezed, I leaned toward the aisle a bit to keep from resting against his arm. As it turned out, this wasn't such a great idea. A couple of the flight attendants were fairly big, too, and as they went up and down the aisle, they kept bumping into my arm with their hips. This happened so many times my arm started to feel a little sore and bruised.

This is not a new experience for me. A couple of years ago, a flight attendant ran over my foot with the drink cart as I slept! That hurt! So you'd better believe it when a little while later, as they were pushing the cart down the aisle, I sat up and made sure all my body parts were inside my "space". It was then that I realized the flight attendant was saying, "Watch your elbows, knees and toes! Elbows, knees and toes! Elbows, knees and toes!"

The gal said it over and over so many times, I really felt as though God was speaking to me through her, saying it enough times to get my attention. It worked! I asked Him, "Ok God – what are You saying about elbows, knees and toes?"

See, years ago, I had a dream. In this dream, my mother and I were in a meat packing plant. There were all kinds of animals on a conveyor belt, and although I don't remember most of the dream, the part I remember clearly was this: as I was attempting to leave that place, there was a pig lying on the ground in front of me like a cat with its two front feet sticking out in front of it. In the dream, I heard a voice coming from somewhere that said, "Watch your ankles!"

I found out later that ankles stand for "FAITH". So when I heard, "Elbows, Knees and Toes" on this flight over and over, it resonated inside of me! This is because it hit me in my spirit: if ANKLES mean FAITH, then ELBOWS, KNEES and TOES must have spiritual meanings as well!

Unfortunately, since we were already up in the air by this time, I was unable to research Elbows, Knees and Toes at that moment. I will tell more about this discovery in Part II of this message, entitled, **"Elbows, Knees and Toes – What you Need to Know!"**

So, I settled in to read my Bible. Instead, I heard the Lord ask me, "Are You Prepared?"

Knowing Him as I do, my knee-jerk reaction was, "Prepared for....What?" I have learned to ask first! The last time He said that to me, He asked me if I was "ready" to stop coloring my hair! Honestly, ladies – who is ever READY to stop coloring her hair?

It turned out it was an exercise in obedience, but more about that some other time.

God is what I call a "picture-God". He speaks through pictures and parables, both in the Bible and today. He gives us prophetic words, dreams and visions, and shows us the things that are to come (John 16:13). Even the Hebrew aleph-bet started out as *pictures*! Because I know this about Him, He began to talk to me about the *pictures* He had just shown me: The Safety Instructions.

It troubled me that hardly anybody else paid attention to the safety instructions when they were given. I guess as a people, we have grown complacent that nothing is going to happen. Planes take off and they land every day, hundreds of times a day. In fact, statistically speaking, there is a higher chance of getting attacked by a shark than being in an airplane accident.

So, it is in the airplane pretty much as it is on the earth today – *hardly anybody on the earth is paying attention to His instructions*! However, WE as the REMNANT, the ELECT, the hand-selected heirs of the Kingdom of God are under additional scrutiny and pressure by the Almighty – because He is depending on US to finish out His end-time plan. He has given us instructions, and fully expects us to pay attention.

So, with that, I will share the message that He gave me on the plane: "Are You Prepared?"

1. **The Lord said that we MUST obey instructions** in this next portion of our earthly adventure with Him, because the Kingdom of Heaven is at hand. The safety instruction card is right in front of us on "the plane", a word-play and a symbol of "His PLAN". He says the instructions are right in front of us, easily within our reach, as close as our hands – both in our Bible, and our open hands, raised and ready to receive from Him! **"From that time Jesus began to preach, and to say, Repent: for *the kingdom of heaven is at hand* (Matthew 4:17 KJV)."**

2. **The Lord spoke to me about the oxygen masks** dropping down in front of us from overhead. What is in the masks? OXYGEN! Air – Pneuma – Ruach - Holy Spirit! Where does it come from? Overhead, from Him – and it's in front of us, and not behind! That's right! When the cabin pressure drops – or, alternatively, since it is an upside down kingdom, when the pressure is ON -- due to some unforeseen circumstance or calamity, the Holy Spirit is on the job! His Name in Hebrew is Ruach HaKodesh – Breath, Life, Spirit. He is the air we breathe!

We must continue to breathe to survive. All we have to do is reach out, take His mask, and BREATHE! A woman when she is birthing will breathe deeply. An athlete as s/he runs breathes deeply. When the adrenaline from our "fight-or-flight" syndrome kicks in, we breathe deeply!

Instead of breathing in "the world", breathe in the Holy Spirit! Instead of breathing in 'panic', breathe in PEACE! Instead of breathing in 'anger', breathe in FORGIVENESS! Breathe Him in deeply. Rest in Him! Know He has your back! Spend time with Him!

Interestingly, *even if the bag doesn't inflate, the oxygen is still flowing*. This means that although it may seem that nothing has changed, be confident that the Holy Spirit *is flowing*, and continue to breathe Him in! Don't stop breathing!

3. **He talked to me about our seat belts: we MUST stay buckled up** for this next segment of our journey. The flight attendant said to keep the seat belt on whenever we are seated, *even if the captain has turned off the "fasten seatbelt" light*; however, she also showed us how to loosen it and release the buckle. I believe the Lord is saying that he wants us to stay put, seated in heavenly places with Him.

"And hath raised us up *together*, and made us *sit together in heavenly places* in *Christ* Jesus... (Ephesians 2:6 KJV)"

Don't get out of your seat! It is the adversary's goal to get you up out of your heavenly seat, to get you out of position. He may flash the "unbuckle-your-seatbelt-sign", like an angel of light that he has been known to be, (see 2 Corinthians 11:14) to lure you. DON'T DO IT! Use your seat belt, keep it buckled up, and stay seated with Him in Heavenly places!

You DO have free will. You can choose to release your buckle at any time, remove your seat belt, stand up, and walk away. God is not going to force you to stay seated with Him in heavenly places. It is a choice. You can get up, *but WHY would you?* Stay in His peace and His rest. Stay in relationship.

4. **That brings us to the exit doors.** I ALWAYS check to see where the nearest exit doors are once I board the aircraft. Why? In case of emergency! I want to know how to get out of a bad situation, should one arise. In life, "diverse trials" (see James 1:2) happen altogether too often, it seems, but God has given us some REALLY good news: **Jesus IS the DOOR!** He is our Exit door, our entrance door, *and* the gatekeeper. He is the Way! He is the Truth! He is the Life! No man comes to the Father except **through** Him!

"Verily, verily, I say unto you, I am the door... (John 10:7 KJV)."

"I am the door: by me if any man enter in, he shall be saved, and shall go in and out, and find pasture (John 10:9)."

"Jesus saith unto him, I am the way, the truth, and the life: no man cometh unto the Father, but by me (John 14:6)."

If you look at the floor of the aircraft, you can see the lighted strips that will direct you to the exit door... even if visibility is poor, even in the dark, even in the midst of the storm, even in smoke and flames! That sure speaks to me! God will light the way! He will direct your path with His word!

"Thy word is a lamp unto my feet, and a light unto my path (Psalm 119:105)."

He gives you a MAP and a Strategy – FOLLOW ME (see Matthew 4:19)! He will lead you by any means necessary to guide you to the Exit Door – straight to Jesus! He will make sure you can find your way to Him: to help, to life, and life more abundantly (see John 10:10).

Aren't you glad you looked for, and found, the "Exit Door"? Lean on that Door! When that Door opens, and it will open as you knock, you will fall right into His arms!

He is also our portal, our entrance into the heavenly realm. He invites us to, "...come up here (Revelation 4:1)", and to "...go in and out (the door) and find pasture (John 10:9)", to spend time with Him in His presence. I have had multiple visions in the last year or so that all start out with that one phrase, "Come up here..." This is because I said, "YES!" to intimacy with Jesus.

I believe in this next segment in time, He will be working on the remnant to grow with Him in even MORE intimate ways! These are our instructions!

On the plane, the Lord asked me, "Are you prepared?" I want to urge you to do a "safety check", and look at the instructions He has given us all:

1. He gives us the instruction manual: the Bible
2. He gives us our own personal line of communication with Him, a "hotline": speaking in tongues;
3. He gives us His own Holy Spirit;
4. He seats us in heavenly places with Him and even shows us the Exit Door from diverse trials!

5. He does all of this in order to prepare us for this life, and more particularly, for what is coming in our immediate futures.

*This safety message brought to you by The Father, The Son and The Holy Spirit.

Blessings and abundance as you SHIFT into this next segment!

CHAPTER SEVEN

FREE YOURSELF UP TO MINISTER IN THIS NEXT GREAT MOVE OF GOD! IT'S HAPPENING NOW!

The Lord gave me a most encouraging word, and He is anxious that I share it with you. It is: **"Free yourself up to minister in this great move of God! It's happening now!"**

In prayer this morning, the Lord showed me a front-end loader dumping its bucket of granite into the back of a pickup truck, over and over again. This is what you have been in training for your entire Life – to carry "The Rock"- JESUS! It is your "job" to fill up, pour out, and fill up again and again with "The Rock"! He is the front-end loader, and You are the pickup truck! Let's get to work!

The Lord says, "I am coming, but not like you expect."

Yesterday morning the Lord gave me two visions of Himself. In one, He was a Lion, walking across a rocky mountain top. He had on His crown, red velvet and gold. We locked gaze periodically as He made His way across the rugged terrain. I knew that He always knew where I was – I was always in His sight. In the other, Jesus was on a white horse on a bed of clouds. He had on His crown and His sash. His horse was magnificent! Its long mane caught my attention, as it pawed at the "ground", first with its left hoof, and then its right. Jesus' horse was anxious to move!

The Lord gave me some very specific instructions for myself, but for all of us, He said (my clarification in parenthesis):

"I am giving you wisdom and a roadmap, a strategy. You have the skills necessary for this (next) great move. I am tempering your will, and your emotions, to stabilize you throughout (this move). That is why you have been in emotional upheaval, to teach you balance, and control."

"I am moving among my people. Some will be pushed into position (pushed to the front lines). Some will be thrust, and some will just POP onto the front (lines) as I move. You move (when) I move and sway among you, and your actual, physical bodies make way for advancement."

As He spoke, I remembered a movie I saw once. It was of the Holy Spirit moving through a crowd in South America somewhere. As He did, He cut a swath, an actual path, through the crowd of people. Human eyes could not see His form, but their bodies sure moved out of the way for Him!

Your Destiny is Guaranteed!

"My hand will be on you, as I push and sift and sort whoever I will - those who will be forerunners for this great move. However, you will all be involved! Maybe not at the very beginning, but you surely will not miss it!"

"You who hear My Voice will all be involved to some degree, at a certain level. This will be revealed to you 'as you go' (see Luke 17:14)."

"Your place has been determined. Your position has been determined. Your advancement has been predetermined, and your Destiny is guaranteed, says the Lord God Jehovah (see Romans 8:29-30)."

"For those whom He foreknew [of whom He was aware and loved beforehand], He also destined from the beginning [foreordaining them] to be molded into the image of His Son [and share inwardly His likeness], that He might become the firstborn among many brethren.

And those whom He thus foreordained, He also called; and those whom He called, He also justified (acquitted, made righteous, putting them into right standing with Himself). And those whom He justified, He also glorified [raising them to a heavenly dignity and condition or state of being]" (Romans 8:29-30)'.

"Every single thing you have ever done, no matter how small or seemingly meaningless, has given you a skill, or honed one you already had, for the great move. You have been in training. Some have learned patience, others control. Some have learned to keep their wits about them, while others learned skills necessary to help others learn what *they* needed to know. Some have been used of Me, unbeknownst to them, to help push, shove or sand and mold others into the shape that I desire."

You are the chosen vessel

"O house of Israel, can I not do with you as this potter does? says the Lord. Behold, as the clay is in the potter's hand, so are you in My hand, O house of Israel" (Jeremiah 18:6).

"This is one great "Potter's Wheel"! The oil is the anointing that I use to shape the clay, on the outside and the inside of the vessel. **You are the chosen vessel and I have made of you what I will for this current season,** for this fragment of time. Every hardship, every joy, has shaped you into what I desire you to be, inside and out. You look marvelous in my eyes."

"I have entrusted you with my greatest treasure – each other. You are shaping and honing each other by the work of my hands. Each act you perform (for the Kingdom) has an effect on every person (ripple effect), and for eternity. Just listen to Me, and you will be in the Book of Acts, just like my beloved Apostles!"

So, if there was any doubt that you are chosen for this move of God, it must be totally gone now!

Be blessed in the Kingdom!

CHAPTER EIGHT

ACCESS TO THE ANOINTING:
THE BRIDE AND THE GUARD

In prayer recently, I went into a vision. I saw myself with my head bowed, surrounded by huge angels. I was so tiny in the center of this circle of enormous angels. As I watched, I started to grow, and grow, and grow, until I was the same size as them! I saw myself turn to walk and my footsteps were loud and crashing. I felt like Gulliver - a giant! I heard God say to me, "You are bigger than you think you are."

I am here to tell you now - You are MUCH bigger than you think you are in the spirit realm! You are a giant among angels. You have incredible authority and earth shattering power! Remember – it is the anointing that breaks the yoke (Is. 10:27). You must learn to access your anointing.

I had a vision of a bride's hand writing on a scroll. I knew it was a bride because of the long white glove that was hooked over one finger. I leaned in to see what was on the scroll, and as she furiously penned her words, writing as quickly as she could, the words looked like music notes; yet, somehow I knew they were Hebrew letters! Suddenly, she stood, and rolled up the scroll. I could see her in all her beauty in her wedding gown. She handed the scroll to "The Guard", and ran out of the room.

The Guard looked like a medieval knight, covered in black armor. He stood motionless against the wall. I thought of the guards at Buckingham Palace – nothing moves them! He stood, as if I wasn't there - his steely, masked face facing straight in front of him.

I turned to the Lord and asked Him what was on the scroll.

He said, "Access to the Anointing!"

I was in awe! "How do I get what is on the scroll? How do I get access to the anointing?"

God said, "ASK The Guard!"

Pondering this, I saw myself walk up to The Guard. I could see the scroll held tightly in his armored fingers, tucked in close to his body. He was guarding and protecting it.

Cocking my head, I timidly said to The Guard, "Can I access the anointing?"

Nothing happened. Not sure I had asked the right way, I thought, "Maybe I needed to DECREE it...or DECLARE it...or even COMMAND him to give it to me."

I opened my mouth, deciding to DECLARE it. The very second that I did, as soon as I heard, "I D..." come out of my mouth, something happened! It was as if I went down a chute, or a slide, and I found myself in another dimension!

In this place, I saw the bride twirling, spinning like a top. I could only see her from above, as if I was looking down at her from the ceiling. I recognized her crown as she spun quickly in place. It was silver with a pewter look to it, and there were strips of metal that hung down from it with symbols on them. As she spun, the centrifugal force made the metal strips lift into the air. I focused on them, and I caught glimpses of the symbols, but they went by so fast that I could only make out a few.

I saw something that looked like an "M" with an apostrophe next to it, and a daisy-flower icon. There was also something similar to a triangle. These icons appeared to be engraved, or embedded, in her crown, and were easily distinguishable; however, she was twirling so quickly that I could only see a few symbols as they sped past.

In searching out these symbols, God showed me these were Hebrew letters. Initially, I couldn't find a Hebrew letter that looked like an "M", but the Spirit of God revealed to me that since I was overhead looking down at her, I was seeing the letter upside down on the crown. The "M" was actually an upside-down SHIN, which looks like a "W". I recognized the apostrophe as a "YOD", and the triangle was a Dalet. The only symbol that I could not find was the flower – there are no Hebrew letters that look like a daisy that I found.

Digging deeper, as I followed this Holy Ghost bread-crumb trail, I located "The Flower of Shushan". It is tied to the Hebrew language, and to its 'aleph-bet'. I cannot get into all the depth of what it means relative to the Hebrew alphabet, because it is deep! Just one of its meanings, however, is that it appeared on pillars that held up buildings in Shushan – at one time the capital of Babylon. This is where Esther and King Xerxes lived, in the city of Shushan (Esther 1:2,5; 2:3; 3:15; 9:11).

Once I found this, I was able to interpret the vision and its symbols. The Hebrew letters and symbols can mean many things, and therefore to him who wishes to dig, much more can be gleaned. However, here are the symbols, with just one of their many meanings, as the Holy Spirit led:

YUD – Work, A Deed, To Make; also, Constancy (when it appears before another letter, as here)

SHIN – To Consume, or to Destroy, as in FIRE (or teeth)

Flower – Symbol upon Pillars (of society, of governmental authority, in the Babylonian culture)

DALET – Door, Pathway, to Enter; Abide

I received a download from Heaven that the letters and symbols engraved on her crown are "medals of honor" – received through battle, forever engraved on her crown! Don't forget: I only saw these four "medals". There were many more that I couldn't see.

I do not pretend to be a Hebrew scholar. All that I do is guided by the Holy Spirit. I believe the Lord was speaking TO His Bride ABOUT His Bride! This is what I believe He was saying:

It is our JOB (our work, our deed – to make ourselves) to constantly be on fire (or to chew up and spit out, to destroy) and consume anything that is attached to the PILLARS (of faith in our lives and in our realms of authority); to stay on the path in order to enter into (through the door) and abide with Him, our Bridegroom, in these quickly accelerating (end) times.

In order to do that, we need to have **ACCESS to the ANOINTING,** because it is the anointing that breaks the yoke (Is. 10:27)! Our Father is teaching us how to access it. In order to get it from the GUARD, (an angel assigned to this task, perhaps, because God is not going to give the anointing to just anybody!), we His Bride, simply must first, BELIEVE, and second,

DECLARE that we have it.

Once we grasp how simple this TRUTH truly is, and get past the LIE of the enemy that we are not anointed, the very instant that we open our mouths to start declaring things, we will be immediately transported into another dimension – the spiritual realm, where we are GIANTS AMONG ANGELS -- and *well able to destroy anything that stands against us!*

Now open your mouth! Declare it!

CHAPTER NINE

THE MANIFESTATIONS OF THE PROMISES OF GOD ARE COMING INTO VIEW!

My husband and I are staying in a waterfront lake-house for the next few days. To get here, we drove for two days from Texas to Ohio, spending half a day in Nashville. After driving for the next eight hours, we arrived late at night. It was dark, and we couldn't see it very well, but we knew the lake was right outside the window. The moon was gorgeous in the sky, and there was a reflection of its light on the waters.

The next morning, I walked out into the living room, not expecting it to be so incredibly bright! The big picture window blasted sunlight into the room. The lake was in full view, peacefully still and shining in all its natural beauty! There were several adult geese and a bunch of babies swimming in a row, immediately in front of the window. As I stood looking at this glorious scene, it hit me: **THE MANIFESTATIONS OF THE PROMISES OF GOD ARE COMING INTO VIEW!**

THE PROMISES HAVE STARTED TO MANIFEST!

The promises have started to manifest! They have started to come true. We have been excitedly awaiting for this trip for months now. We have worked on every detail, constructing it right down to our housing and food. Time was all that separated us from it, and now, it is finally here!

In the same way, there is construction being done on the dam that contains the lake. Because of this construction, there is a chain link fence that separates all the lake houses from it. It is designated a construction zone. We can SEE the lake through the fence; we can SMELL it, we can even HEAR it - we just cannot TOUCH it from the exact spot where we are, in this particular house.

This spoke to me! The lake symbolizes our promises – they are right in front of us! We can see them, we can smell them, some can even hear them. We just cannot touch them - YET! And that is a mighty big YET!! However, the lake has come into view, and so have our promises from God!

SIGNS FOR GOD'S PEOPLE

Hanging on the fence are construction signs: "DANGER: Authorized Personnel Only" and "EMERGENCY PERSONNEL ONLY". Both of these signs speak to AUTHORITY! All of us at this level are AUTHORIZED PERSONNEL, so enter in! However, for some of us, our specific promises are still under construction. Some promises require us to use our authority to remove the obstacles – the fences -- that are keeping them from manifesting in the natural realm. Regardless, there is only a very thin veil, a "see-through" fence, between all of us and our promises! They are on their way! Use your Authority!

Your Personal Protective Equipment is an OFF-FENCE-IVE weapon!

There is another sign that says, "PPE REQUIRED BEYOND THIS

POINT". PPE stands for Personal Protective Equipment. For us as God's people, this means *SHIELDS UP! SWORDS UP!* Get that hard hat on – the helmet of truth! Get your protective gear on, and don't take it off! **Your Personal Protective Equipment is an OFF-FENCE-IVE weapon!** Use your PPE constantly, and consistently!

In between the fence and the lake is a dry dirt road, maybe only 20-30 feet across. Each day, there is a water truck that comes and sprays water on it to keep the dust down. This water truck symbolizes the Holy Spirit coming daily to water the word in you!

There is only this one, last, little stretch of desert highway, this one little patch of dry, dirt road that stands between us and our lake of promises! Do not grow weary in well-doing, because in the end, we still win! YOU STILL WIN!

"And let us not be weary in well doing: for in due season we shall reap, if we faint not," **(Gal. 6:9).**

Beyond this "fence" are promises that are as yet still dammed up, behind a fence. Some are still under construction, and require us to use our authority and our spiritual weapons to pull them into the natural realm, and our lives. However, God is faithful to complete the good work that He has begun. He is manifesting His promises into the NOW!

"And I am convinced and sure of this very thing, that He Who began a good work in you will continue until the day of Jesus Christ [right up to the time of His return], developing [that good work] and perfecting and bringing it to full completion in you," **(Phil. 1:6).**

Watch for it: His promises are manifesting right in front of our eyes! They have come into view!

CHAPTER TEN

NEXT GENERATION REFORMATION TEAM!

I had an exciting dream recently of horses and riders racing together as a team. In it, I believe that the Lord has revealed a few things about those that are called to be the next generation reformation team!

In this dream, I am a watcher. There are several horses with riders, lined up in a row. I get the impression they are a team, lining up for the start of some type of a horse show or other kind of contest, like the Olympics. With heads bowed, so I am unable to see their faces, in unison, the riders all make a hand-signal, passing their hand over their heads. It looks like the signal for "cutting off" something, using their hand as a knife or a sword.

The horses start to race, and the riders all stand up on the backs of the horses. "The Camera" zooms in for a close-up, and I am shown one of the riders' faces. A woman, 30-something, with brown hair, has her eyes closed. I feel she is full of faith and trust. There is a hint of a veil or a scarf blowing in the wind.

"The Camera" zooms way out, allowing the watcher to see the big picture. They are running on the top of the outside wall of a castle, on a mountain top. It's only a thin ledge, with no guard-rail or safety net of any kind. The castle is made of salt, and is on the very top of a mountain, also made of salt.

One of the horses runs into the back of another, a black one with a rider dressed in black, forcing him off the ledge. The horse stops briefly – as if he will recover his footing – but then loses it and slides down the mountain. The horse finally stops part of the way down, but the rider goes over its head, down the side of the mountain. As he falls, the rider cries out, "Oh, my God! Oh, my God!" I also heard him saying something about salt, but I didn't catch it.

INTERPRETATION:

At the beginning, the riders are lined up side by side, a team. They all have their heads bowed to the Lord. ALL make the same hand movement simultaneously, in unison –cutting off ties to the world.

The woman is the next generation bride – she is "thirty-something", a generation full of faith and trust in the Lord. They are blinded to all else other than His truth, and stand on it!

The salt mountain is the mountain of God, with His Kingdom at the top. The chosen ones are racing along on the ledge of this wall. Webster's 1828 dictionary defines LEDGE as, "A prominent part; a regular part rising or projecting beyond the rest." The Lord is describing the next generation as a ledge – those who rise and project "beyond the rest". It is also a narrow ledge! These enter through the narrow gate, and not the wide road (see Matthew 7:13).

This dream is an apostolic picture of the next generation reformation team! It is a picture of those who have vowed to uphold the word of God, indeed, the KINGDOM OF GOD...to fight for it, and to stand on it. It is where the race is run, together, in unison, with eyes closed in blind faith.

There are those who have somehow illegally gotten to this place of prominence. They have entered by another door.

"Truly, truly, I say to you, he who does not enter the sheepfold by the door but climbs in by another way, that man is a thief and a robber" (John 10:1 ESV).

The next generation remnant's authority will bounce them off the mountain of God, pushing them out the door, leading to their very public spiritual, and in some cases occupational, demise. They will be crying out for mercy, shouting, "My God! My God!"

Yet, even then, they will still be claiming salt all the way down as they fall. About these, Jesus declares he will say, "Get away from me, you evil doer! I never knew you!"

"And then will I declare to them, 'I never knew you; depart from me, you workers of lawlessness'" (Matthew 7:23 ESV).

However, notice in the dream that the horse does not go off the mountain completely – only the rider. God's word stands forever in heaven!

"Forever, O Lord, Your word is settled in heaven [stands firm as the heavens]" (Ps. 119:89 AMPC).

His authority is a vehicle, to be used by permission with wisdom and discernment, given to those whom He chooses. He may allow others to use it for a season – but eventually, wrong doctrine and lies are the doctrine of demons, and God cannot allow it forever. As my mother always says, "God cannot bless Sin!"

"But the [Holy] Spirit distinctly and expressly declares that in latter times some will turn away from the faith, giving attention to deluding and seducing spirits and doctrines that demons teach, Through the hypocrisy and pretensions of liars whose consciences are seared (cauterized), ... " (1 Timothy 4:1-2 AMPC)

The next generation reformation team is here. They ruthlessly chase truth. Nothing but Jesus will do. Their eyes are closed to falsehood and their ears open only to His voice. Their authority and anointing is so far beyond what we have seen to date! It will be the Church of Acts all over again!

It will be exciting times for those who are in this generation and beyond,

"For I tell you that many prophets and kings desired to see what you see, and did not see it, and to hear what you hear, and did not hear it" (Luke 10:24 ESV).

Many blessings as we step into this next generation reformation!

ABOUT THE AUTHOR

Edie Bayer
Kingdom Promoters – Promoting the Kingdom of God
www.KingdomPromoters.org
www.EdieBayer.com
Edie@KingdomPromoters.org

Edie Bayer is an author, a speaker and travelling minister. Edie's primary call is to promote others that are ministering in the Kingdom of God, creating unity instead of a spirit of competition. Edie believes that we are to "complete and not compete"!

Edie can be found on TBN, and is a backup TV show host for two television programs on Destiny TV.

Edie is a frequent contributor to prophetic newsletters: The Elijah List (www.ElijahList.com), Spirit Fuel (www.SpiritFuel.me), and Women of Impact Ministries (www.womenofimpactministries.com).

Edie believes that EVERYBODY has a book in them – and it's TIME to write it! Her most recent assignment from God is to help other Christian authors pen their novels and texts. She helps budding authors accomplish their goals with her workshop entitled, *"Write That Book! You Have a Book in You – Now Write It!"* Edie teaches this workshop by invitation around the country.

Along with her husband, Darryl, Edie is co-founder of Kingdom Promoters www.KingdomPromoters.org). Kingdom Promoters is a 501(C)(3) Non-Profit Organization. Kingdom Promoters' mission statement is "To promote the Kingdom of God, and to promote the people who promote the Kingdom of God!" This ministry works to further God's Kingdom by acting as an incubator to assist fledgling ministries in their start-up stages and promote those who are promoting the kingdom of God. Kingdom Promoters also hosts itinerant speakers and travelling ministers.

Please visit Edie's websites: www.KingdomPromoters.org and www.EdieBayer.com for more information about Edie Bayer, books, CD's and DVD's, as well as how to bring Edie to your church, fellowship, retreat, ministry or group!

www.ingramcontent.com/pod-product-compliance
Lightning Source LLC
Chambersburg PA
CBHW071851020426
42331CB00007B/1963